At Issue

| Teen Driving

Other Books in the At Issue Series:

At Issue

|Teen Driving

Michele Siuda Jacques, Book Editor

GREENHAVEN PRESS
A part of Gale, Cengage Learning

Detroit • New York • San Francisco • New Haven, Conn • Waterville, Maine • London

GALE
CENGAGE Learning®

Elizabeth Des Chenes, *Director, Publishing Solutions*

© 2013 Greenhaven Press, a part of Gale, Cengage Learning.

Gale and Greenhaven Press are registered trademarks used herein under license.

For more information, contact:
Greenhaven Press
27500 Drake Rd.
Farmington Hills, MI 48331-3535
Or you can visit our Internet site at gale.cengage.com

For product information and technology assistance, contact us at

Gale Customer Support, 1-800-877-4253
For permission to use material from this text or product, submit all requests online at www.cengage.com/permissions.

Further permissions questions can be e-mailed to permissionrequest@cengage.com.

Articles in Greenhaven Press anthologies are often edited for length to meet page requirements. In addition, original titles of these works are changed to clearly present the main thesis and to explicitly indicate the author's opinion. Every effort is made to ensure that Greenhaven Press accurately reflects the original intent of the authors. Every effort has been made to trace the owners of copyrighted material.

Cover photograph © Images.com/Corbis.

LIBRARY OF CONGRESS CATALOGING-IN-PUBLICATION DATA

Teen driving / Michele Siuda Jacques
    p. cm. -- (At issue)
    Summary: "Teen Driving: Books in this anthology series focus a wide range of viewpoints onto a single controversial issue, providing in-depth discussions by leading advocates, a quick grounding in the issues, and a challenge to critical thinking skills"-- Provided by publisher.
    Includes bibliographical references and index.
    ISBN 978-0-7377-6418-5 (hardback) -- ISBN 978-0-7377-6419-2 (paperback)
    1. Teenage automobile drivers--United States. 2. Traffic safety--United States. I. Jacques, Michele Siuda.
    HE5620.J8T4382 2012
    388.3'2108350973--dc23
                                                                 2012012541

Printed in the United States of America
1 2 3 4 5 6 7 16 15 14 13 12

Contents

Introduction

Car crashes are the number one cause of death among teens in the United States. Despite an increase in seat belt use and a decrease in drunken driving, the fatality rate for drivers aged sixteen to nineteen is four times that of drivers aged twenty-five to sixty-nine, a study by the Children's Hospital of Philadelphia and State Farm Insurance Companies found.

The greatest threat to teen drivers is inexperience. Every state now has a graduated driver licensing program, which slows a teenager's push into the real world of driving solo. But a study in the *Journal of the American Medical Association* found that restrictions on passengers and nighttime driving have not cut into the fatality rate for older teens. It is believed that older teens simply delay getting their license or are not getting enough experience on their learner's and intermediate permits to handle more challenging driving conditions.

What is clear is that driver education classes are not enough. Often, an instructor merely focuses on teaching students what they need to know to pass a test, not what they need to know to navigate an icy passage late at night, for example. "Despite widespread appeal of driver education, scientific evaluations indicate that it does not produce safer drivers," the National Highway Traffic Safety Administration said in a 2009 report.

A greater emphasis, too, has been placed on parents and the role they can play in influencing their child when they are behind the wheel. Parents who focus on driving instead of texting, talking on the phone, eating, or other distracting behaviors set the example for their teens who are tempted with distractions while driving. "The single easiest way to teach your kids to drive is to drive the way you want them to drive," said Mike Speck, lead instructor at Ford Driving Skills for

Life. Driving with a parent provides a safe environment for an inexperienced driver to make mistakes and learn from them. A study by the American Automobile Association (AAA), however, found that many teens and parents were not driving nearly as much and in as varied of conditions as experts had hoped. Many experts recommend that parents spend time teaching their children to drive in hazardous conditions such as during fog and iciness, as well as late at night and on freeways.

A study by AAA of beginning drivers in North Carolina found that 57 percent of the crashes in which a teen was to blame involved three main mistakes: failure to reduce speed, inattention, and failure to yield. Most of these mistakes resolve themselves with experience. In addition, Children's Hospital of Philadelphia and State Farm found that 75 percent of fatal accidents caused by teens were linked to these mistakes: driving too fast for the road conditions or weather; not scanning the road to identify what was coming ahead or from the side, and being distracted by something inside or outside the vehicle. Technology often proves to be a deadly distraction. Nearly 28 percent of all vehicle crashes can be linked to talking on a cell phone or texting while driving, says the National Safety Council.

Distractions are not just of the technological variety. Having just one friend in the car increases the risk of a crash for a teen driver. Teens very much want to be accepted by their peers and the pressure to speed and take other risks can be too much for a young driver to resist. The teenage brain is undergoing great change that can impair reasoning and decision making just when an adolescent needs most to be exhibiting impulse control. This explains why otherwise conscientious kids will make surprisingly poor judgment calls.

Parents, insurance companies, safety experts, and others agree that teen drivers improve with experience. The authors in *At Issue: Teen Driving* explore graduated licensing programs and other efforts to help new drivers.

1

Federal Graduated Driver Licensing Would Reduce Teen Crashes

Lori Johnston

Lori Johnston writes business and employment stories for publications such as the Atlanta Journal-Constitution, Atlanta Business Chronicle, *Bankrate.com,* Atlanta Homes & Lifestyles, *and* Developer *magazine.*

Legislation to cut down on teen car crashes and high insurance rates is winding its way through Congress. Every state has some form of graduated driver licensing, but federal provisions would bring all states in line with recommendations supported by groups such as the National Transportation Safety Board and the American Academy of Pediatrics. The requirements include three stages of licensing, passenger limits, late-night driving limits, and bans on the use of cell phones and other distracting devices.

Teens wanting to get fast and furious behind the wheel would have to wait a little longer to pack the car with friends or make late-night runs to the movies under legislation pending in Congress.

Although it might annoy teens seeking car keys and independence, the "graduated driver's licensing" effort in Congress could combat the No. 1 killer of U.S. teens: car crashes. More than 10 American teens die each day, on average, in car crashes. In August 2011, for example, four high school football players died in an accident in New Jersey.

Decreasing Crashes and Insurance Rates

The legislation seeks to establish minimum requirements in states for graduated licensing laws, which phase in full driving privileges by age 18. If passed, insurers expect the predicted reduction in teen crashes would keep auto insurance rates from rising or even cause a slight decrease.

The proposal is making its way through congressional committees. Its best chance of getting passed is as a part of the multibillion-dollar federal transportation bill, says Jacqueline Gillan, president of Advocates for Highway and Auto Safety, a member of the Saferoads4teens Coalition. The coalition comprises insurance, consumer, safety, medical and other organizations pushing for a national standard for graduated licensing laws.

> [The] STANDUP Act is a vaccination to protect teens in a very high-risk and very potentially fatal environment.

Aiming to Stop Teen Crashes

Every state has some type of graduated driver's licensing. However, few have all of the provisions included in the federal proposal, which is supported by organizations such as the National Transportation Safety Board, the federal Centers for Disease Control and Prevention, the American Academy of Pediatrics and the Insurance Institute for Highway Safety.

Research has found that states with graduated driver's licensing programs have seen anywhere from a 20 percent to 40 percent decrease in crashes involving 16- and 17-year-old drivers. . . .

Only one state, New Jersey, already is in full compliance with the federal proposal. Several other states—Arkansas,

Connecticut, Delaware, District of Columbia, Indiana, Kentucky, Maine, New Mexico, New York, North Carolina, Rhode Island and Tennessee—would need to make just one or two changes in existing laws to be in compliance, Gillan says.

Graduated licensing laws keep beginners out of high-risk situations during the early stages of driving, says Emily Pukala, a spokeswoman for Allstate.

The federal STANDUP (Safe Teen and Novice Driver Uniform Protection) Act would establish these minimum requirements for states:

- Three-stage license process: Learner's permit at 16, followed by an intermediate stage, then all restrictions lifted at 18.

- Passenger limits: No more than one non-family passenger under 21, unless a licensed driver over 21 is in the vehicle (learner's permit and intermediate stages).

- Bans on non-emergency use of cellphones and other devices, including text messaging (learner's permit and intermediate stages).

- Late-night driving limits: A curfew would be set for driving (learner's permit and intermediate stages).

"It would almost be as if we had a cure for cancer and we gave it to the states and said, 'Whenever you feel like it, we want you to distribute it to your population,'" Gillan says. "This STANDUP Act is a vaccination to protect teens in a very high-risk and very potentially fatal environment."

Setting Limits

A total of $25 million in grants will be available to states that comply with minimum requirements set by the STANDUP Act within three years of the federal law being enacted. States that meet those requirements will split that amount, which could be used to help enforce the law.

Sanctions are modeled after other laws such as the one in 1984 that established 21 as the minimum drinking age nationally. States that don't follow the graduated licensing requirements within three years of its enactment would lose federal highway funding, up to 10 percent.

An Allstate survey found that nearly six in 10 Americans favor a federal law that would establish minimum requirements for graduated driver's licensing.

The survey also found that:

- 66 percent back a minimum age of 16 to receive a learner's permit.

- 69 percent favor requiring three stages of licensing.

- 70 percent support restricting unsupervised nighttime driving for those under 18.

- 65 percent support restricting the number of non-family passengers for drivers under 18.

- 81 percent favor a ban on talking on cellphones or texting while driving for younger drivers.

Steering Teens Away from Danger

During Thanksgiving break in 2009, Andrew Case, 17, and five friends were heading to a movie theater in a Honda SUV on a rainy evening. About 8:45 p.m., the car, driven by a 16-year-old, crashed on a road in Pottstown, Pa., killing Andrew and another teen.

"The boy that was driving dropped his cellphone and bent down to pick it up. He lost control," says Andrew's mother, Marlene Case.

The driver had had his license for only about three weeks.

"I just don't think that their brains are developed enough to make these critical decisions. They're just too young, too immature," Case says.

Case's son was one of more than 5,600 people killed in crashes involving drivers ages 15 to 20 in 2009.

Graduated licensing requirements would bolster parents' efforts to set rules such as limiting the number of unlicensed passengers, says Case, an emergency room nurse.

"If there were less kids in the car, that's the main thing. If the laws are in place, the kids might say, 'Oh, hey maybe we shouldn't do this.'" Case says.

Gillan adds: "Who wants to say, 'No, my mom won't let me.' It's much easier to say, 'No, it's the law and I can't do it.'"

2

Graduated Driver Licensing Fails to Reduce Fatal Crashes

Genevra Pittman

Genevra Pittman reports on health and the environment and has written for Reuters Health, the Boston Globe, *and* OnEarth, *the magazine of the Natural Resources Defense Council.*

Graduated driver licensing has not proven effective in reducing crashes among older teens. Car crashes account for more than one-third of US teen deaths, according to the Centers for Disease Control and Prevention, and are the leading cause of death for teenagers. By placing restrictions on young drivers, the aim of allowing teens to gradually ramp up their responsibility on the road may be backfiring. Researchers say keeping younger drivers off the road limits their experience and puts them at risk when they are no longer under driving restrictions.

Programs that keep young drivers from taking the wheel at night, or with a car full of teens, may reduce the risk of fatal crashes in some drivers—but increase that risk in others.

A study that compared death rates found fewer fatal crashes among 16-year-olds, but more among 18-year-olds, when states had so-called graduated driver licensing programs in place. And there was no difference in fatal crashes among all teen drivers combined under the programs.

Teens "learn well and react well," said Jean Shope, from the University of Michigan Transportation Research Institute.

Figuring out the best way to start them driving, she told Reuters Health, is "quite challenging. If we want teens to get driving experience while they're teens, we have to face the fact that they are teenagers and still have development issues going on."

Car crashes account for more than one-third of deaths in U.S. teens, according to the Centers for Disease Control and Prevention, and are the leading cause of death for that age group.

Starting in 1996, states began putting restrictions on drivers under 18, including on what hours they could take the wheel (not after midnight, for example) and who they could have as a passenger (no more than one other teenager). Now, every state has some degree of a graduated driver-licensing program.

To test their effect on all teen drivers, researchers led by Scott Masten from the California Department of Motor Vehicles combined data on fatal crashes in adolescents ages 16 to 19 between 1986 and 2007.

Restrictions Help Some Teens, but Not All

On the whole, fewer teens died in car crashes when stricter driving policies were in place. With no driving restrictions, about 47 of every 100,000 teens died in a car crash every year, on average. With strict programs, including both nighttime driving and passenger restrictions, that decreased to 30 in every 100,000 per year.

When the researchers accounted for other factors, including how often people drove in each state and in what season car crashes occurred, they found that 16-year-olds were 26 percent less likely to die in a crash when states had strict driving restrictions than when they had none.

However, 18-year-olds—who no longer faced the restrictions—were 12 percent more likely to have a fatal crash.

There was no difference in fatal crash rates for 17- or 19-year olds.

And statistical tests couldn't confirm any difference in crashes among all 16- to 19-year-olds combined, with or without the driving policies, Masten and colleagues report in the *Journal of the American Medical Association*.

Based on those findings, they calculated that since 1996, graduated driving licensing programs have been linked to 1,348 fewer fatal crashes in 16-year-old drivers and 1,086 more of those deaths in 18-year-olds.

Other studies generally haven't shown an uptick in crashes in older teens under the licensing programs, researchers say—but that doesn't mean it's not a possible consequence.

Researchers still need to tease out whether driving restrictions help teens drive more safely—or whether they just take them off the road, without necessarily improving behavior and future driving.

Shope, who was not involved in the new study, said that some experts have wondered whether more young drivers will wait to get their licenses until they turn 18 to avoid restrictions that only apply to younger teens.

Another possibility is that even teens who get a license earlier will have less experience driving alone and under challenging conditions when they hit 18, said Dr. Motao Zhu, who studies traffic injuries at West Virginia University.

Researchers still need to tease out whether driving restrictions help teens drive more safely—or whether they just take them off the road, without necessarily improving behavior and future driving, said Pinar Karaca-Mandic, a health economist from the University of Minnesota.

The new findings don't mean that graduated driver licensing programs aren't working, researchers emphasized. They just show there's room for more research, and more policy tweaking.

"We definitely don't want to scrap these programs," Masten told Reuters Health, adding that the findings are also limited because they only include fatal crashes, not more minor accidents.

Anne McCartt, from the Insurance Institute for Highway Safety in Arlington, Virginia, and the author of a commentary on the new study, said that national trends have generally shown a drop in teen crashes since restrictions went into effect.

Previous studies have also suggested benefits from pushing back the age that teens can get their license and requiring supervised driving with an adult, she added.

"I think these studies may help us identify ways to make teens even safer, but we've been doing a much better job than we used to," McCartt told Reuters Health.

3

Graduated Driver Licensing Should Be More Restrictive

Bernie DeGroat

Bernie DeGroat is a media and public relations representative at the University of Michigan.

Despite the prevalence of graduated driver licensing programs, teen drivers remain at great risk for vehicle crashes. States should place restrictions on all interacting risk factors, such as driving at night, driving on weekends, and driving with passengers.

Although most states now have graduated licensing for teen drivers, such programs should be even more restrictive, according to a study by the [University of Michigan] Transportation Research Institute (UMTRI).

"Motor vehicle crashes are the greatest single health threat to teens," says UMTRI researcher C. Raymond Bingham. "Little or no positive change has occurred in teen crash numbers in the past 10–15 years. Clearly, current measures aimed at curbing teen drivers' involvement in crashes are not sufficient."

Bingham and colleagues Jean Shope, Julie Parow and Trivellore Raghunathan studied data from nearly 7,000 teen drivers, Michigan State Police crash records and Michigan Secretary of State driver history records from 1989–96, to identify crash types for which teen drivers are at excess risk, and analyzed psychosocial and behavioral factors that predict crash types.

By calculating crash rates using miles driven by an individual driver, instead of the more common vehicle miles driven, or by using per population methods, the researchers are able to provide a greater degree of specificity with regard to individual travel behavior and exposure to crash risk for men and women in different age groups. In addition, they examined multiple characteristics of car accidents to create more realistic crash types and to measure their effect on risk.

Risk Factors

Teens are at excess risk, they say, for all crash types, which include a combination of various elements: characteristics of the teen driver, time of day, day of week, driver behavior and the context within the vehicle.

"Inexperience, underdeveloped driving skills and immaturity together contribute to poor performance of driving tasks," Bingham says. "Teens are about two-and-a-half times more likely to be in a crash than adults, but certain factors result in large increases in risk.

Most states have passenger and night-time driving restrictions for teens, but none limit driving on weekends.

"One of these is having passengers. From other research, we know it is actually other teen passengers that pose the greatest risk, and we know that each additional passenger results in additional increase in crash risk."

Bingham and colleagues say that driving on weekends and at night are the next most common characteristics of teen driving that increase their crash risk. And when these things happen simultaneously—driving on a weekend night with passengers—they collectively contribute to substantial increases in risk.

Most states have passenger and night-time driving restrictions for teens, but none limit driving on weekends. Graduated driver licensing programs, the researchers say, should place restrictions on all of these interacting factors.

Gender Differences

The researchers found that 56 percent of teen drivers in their study had been in at least one crash, but crash rates improved significantly as the teens gained more driving experience. Women, both teen and adult, have higher crash rates than men for all crash types, except those involving alcohol.

The difference between teenage and adult women's crash rates, however, is smaller than between teen and adult men for all crash types.

Females at age 16 are 3.7 times more likely to be in a crash than adult women drivers ages 45–65, but at age 19 are only 1.2 times more likely. For male drivers, 16-year-olds are 5.1 times more likely to be in a crash than adult men 45–65, but the rate drops to 1.6 times more likely at age 19.

The study also looked at predictors of crash involvement for teen drivers. The best predictor for males was alcohol misuse in the past year. Measures most commonly predictive for females included peer alcohol use, parental permissiveness toward teen alcohol use, susceptibility to peer pressure and alcohol misuse in the past year.

"Some of the measures used may be indicators of the individuals' risk level and their susceptibility to crash involvement," Bingham says. "Other variables, such as alcohol misuse, may contribute directly to increased risk of being involved in a motor vehicle crash, as well. These characteristics might be used to identify teens who are at excess risk of being in a motor vehicle crash, or to tailor interventions to reduce their crash risk."

4

Earlier School Start Times Endanger Teen Drivers

Ellin Holohan

Ellin Holohan is a reporter for HealthDay, an online news service.

Two studies correlated sleep to a decrease in crash rates among teen drivers. In one, earlier school start times made it more likely that teens in one Virginia city would be in a car crash rather than teens in a neighboring city. Biologically, teens are wired to stay up later while still needing to get at least nine hours of sleep a night. When the alarm clock goes off earlier, teens awake sleep deprived just as they are expected to function at a high level as students and as drivers, often with calamitous results.

Starting the school day earlier may lead to more car accidents involving teenagers, new research suggests.

The study, which looked at schools in two cities in Virginia with different start times, found an association between earlier classes and more crashes among sleep-deprived students.

"Teenagers need over nine hours sleep a night, and it looks like a large number of teens don't get sufficient sleep . . . part of that relates to the time that high schools begin," said study author Dr. Robert Vorona, an associate professor of internal medicine in the Division of Sleep Medicine at Eastern Virginia Medical School in Norfolk, Va.

The findings were to be presented Wednesday [in June 2010] at the annual meeting of the American Academy of Sleep Societies, in San Antonio [Texas].

"There are data that demonstrate that lack of sleep has negative consequences for teens," he said. "And some data show that younger drivers are more likely to have crashes when they have inadequate sleep."

The study compared crash rates in 2008 for high school students with widely varying school starting times in Virginia Beach and Chesapeake, two adjacent cities with similar demographics. Virginia Beach's classes started at 7:20 a.m.; Chesapeake's began at 8:40 a.m.

Stark Differences in Crash Rates

While the overall accident rate for all drivers was higher in Virginia Beach, the difference between teens in the two cities was stark, Vorona said. Chesapeake had 46.2 crashes for every 1,000 teen drivers, compared to 65.4 per 1,000 teen drivers in Virginia Beach—a 41% difference.

The statistics are significant, Vorona said, even though they did not prove a direct relationship between school starting times and roadway safety.

"We think the Virginia Beach students may be sleep-deprived," said Vorona, "and that is perhaps the reason for the increased crashes."

Vorona said that the amount of sleep teens get largely depends on what time they get up in the morning.

"They tend to go to bed later no matter what time they get up," said Vorona. Other research shows teens who start school later get more sleep.

He recommended high schools look at starting the day later.

Beyond the impact on driving, early start times probably affect other important areas, Vorona said, calling for research on how they affect teenagers' moods, tardiness and academic performance.

"If you think about something like calculus, we're asking teens to perform complicated mental functions when their minds are probably not fully alert yet," he said.

Dr. Barbara Phillips, of the University of Kentucky College of Medicine, agreed.

When teens increased their sleep, crash rates declined 16.5% during a period when teen crash rates throughout the state increased by 7.8%.

Teens are "biologically programmed" to get sleepy and wake up later than adults, said Phillips, a professor with the school's division of pulmonary, critical care and sleep medicine.

"They truly can't help it. They're just not going to get sleepy at 10 p.m., so it's hard for them to get the eight to 10 hours of sleep they need to get when they have to catch the 7:30 bus."

Phillips is co-author of a study that compared car crash rates and increased sleep for adolescent drivers in Lexington, Ky., when the school district instituted a later school day in 1998. Data were analyzed from the two years before and after the change.

Increased Sleep Helps

The study found that when teens increased their sleep, crash rates declined 16.5% during a period when teen crash rates throughout the state increased by 7.8%.

"Younger, inexperienced drivers don't fare well with additional handicaps such as impaired alertness caused by having to get up earlier than is natural for them," said Phillips. She noted that schools often resist starting the school day later because it affects bus schedules, sports and other after-school activities.

"Changing high school start times is important and difficult," she said. "It can't happen without commitment and work on the part of parents and school officials. Teens are not in a position to set their schedules. We need to help them."

5

Peers Influence Risky Teen Driving

Joseph P. Allen and B. Bradford Brown

Joseph P. Allen is the director of the Virginia Institute of Development of Adulthood at the University of Virginia, an organization that studies how young people grow, how they are influenced by peers and by other social interactions, and how they manage their relationships. He is also a professor of psychology at the University of Virginia, specializing in adolescent social development. B. Bradford Brown is a professor of educational psychology at the University of Wisconsin–Madison and an expert on teenage social development.

Teens, their peers, and motor vehicles can be the perfect storm for poor choices. Teens drive faster and take more risks when they are with their peers. Much of this is due to their desire to be accepted. Complicate the preoccupation with social status with a teen's inability to properly assess risk and rein in impulses, and it can be a deadly combination. Young adults can influence their friends both inside and outside the vehicle in ways that are obvious and not so obvious.

In studies of adolescents and driving, two consistent facts stand out: Motor-vehicle crashes constitute the leading cause of death among teenagers and, contrary to the situation with adults, crash rates and fatalities rise dramatically when teen drivers are accompanied by peer passengers. These facts underscore the need to pay closer attention to the ways in which peers influence teen driving behavior.

Adults understand that, for teenagers, the motor vehicle is more than a mode of transportation. Driving provides not only a degree of autonomy from parental surveillance, but also achievement of a societal status (a driver's license) not open to children and younger adolescents. Adults, however, seem less aware that the motor vehicle constitutes an important social context for teenagers, a factor that is especially pertinent when it comes to concerns about peer influences on teen driving. Researchers recognize that adolescents' driving behavior depends on who is in the car with them. Teenagers drive faster and take more risks when carrying peers than when carrying adults as passengers, especially if the peers are young men. Yet the reasons for these different driving patterns have not been explored. One would expect an adult passenger, typically a parent or older sibling, to act as copilot, giving advice and making the driver aware of real or potential dangers in the road ahead. But if the car is an arena for social interaction, peer passengers are less likely to take on the cautionary copilot role. . . .

Adolescence is characterized in part by the propensity toward engaging in risky and deviant behavior.

Developmental Risk Factors

Adolescence, a unique phase of the lifespan, is relevant to driving in many respects. Teenagers' brains differ from those of adults. On the one hand, teenagers may be less adept at judging risk and inhibiting impulses; on the other, they process multiple forms of information significantly more quickly than do most older adults. Perhaps more important, however, teens also differ in terms of their social development in at least three ways that make them uniquely vulnerable to peer influences on their driving.

Propensity Toward Risky Behavior

Adolescence is characterized in part by the propensity toward engaging in risky and deviant behavior. . . . With conventional means of appearing to be adults unavailable for many teens (e.g., marriage, adult jobs), risky behaviors are one means of establishing that one is no longer a child. Equally important, the striving to establish one's autonomy vis-à-vis parents and to turn increasingly to peers is a fundamental feature of adolescence across many mammalian species. Unfortunately, violating parental rules, behaving unconventionally, and demonstrating comfort with risk-taking behavior all serve these natural developmental goals and, not coincidentally, enhance the likelihood of risky driving.

Universality of Desire to Please Peers

Popular portrayals of adolescents succumbing to peer pressure typically depict an insecure adolescent . . . trying hard to please others so as to "fit in." While this image no doubt captures one important aspect of peer influence, the problem is far broader. Although less-well-adjusted teens do in fact appear more likely to give in to peer pressure, teens who are better adjusted and more popular actually appear highly susceptible to other forms of peer influence, such as peer values. For example, levels of alcohol use and minor deviance tend to increase significantly among popular teens across adolescence, relative to their less popular peers. In most other respects, popular teens look quite well adjusted socially. But relative to their less popular peers, popular teens' alcohol use is actually more closely tied to their peers' values toward this behavior. In brief, although popular teens may not be as susceptible to direct-pressuring behaviors from peers, they are nonetheless quite susceptible to other forms of peer influence. When it comes to peer influence in adolescence, it appears that no one is immune.

Social Danger in the Driving Situation

Although most people are aware of the physical danger teens face when driving with peers (i.e., injuries or death in crashes), they may not recognize that driving also entails one specific context in which a potentially large social threat— damage to peer relationships and peer status—can play out. As adolescents maneuver down a highway with their peers in the car, they are not simply trying to drive safely; they are also trying to maintain and strengthen critical peer relationships. . . . All available evidence suggests that adolescents' preoccupation with their social status is neither needless nor irrational; in some ways, it is a matter of survival. To intervene in a way that has an impact, it will be important to move beyond any temptation to trivialize this very real adolescent need. Although not all social pressures in adolescence are directed toward deviant or risky behaviors, it is nevertheless true that teens in cars are, at times, literally balancing immediate and pressing concerns about maintaining their social standing (which has clear, long-term implications for their social and emotional survival) against risks to their physical survival that appear far more distant and vague.

Driving Is a Unique Situation

The risk factors described above would apply to most situations of peer influence toward deviant behavior. Unfortunately, the act of driving an automobile creates several additional factors likely to enhance any peer influences.

Lack of Visual Cues

Teen drivers are placed in a position where they cannot face or look at those pressuring them. Without these visual cues, it is difficult to tell whether peers are serious, joking, angry, or rejecting (e.g., is a suggestion to "floor it" meant seriously or not). In addition, teens are simply in a fundamentally weaker position to be carrying out any negotiation if they can be seen by, but cannot see, those with whom they are negotiating.

Divided Attention

Teens must try to fend off peer pressure and maintain their status in the peer group while being forced to devote most of their concentration to an entirely unrelated task (driving). Each of these tasks can, at times, require almost undivided attention for successful execution.

Peers of teen drivers get a literal and figurative free ride on many of the risky behaviors they suggest.

Forced Conventionality

Given that behaving unconventionally can be a way to establish credibility within a peer group, the requirement as a driver to behave at all times in a very conventional manner creates a significant social burden on the teen driver. For example, everyone else can act silly or crazy, if that's what the group is calling for, but the driver can't.

Peer "Free Ride"

Peers of teen drivers get a literal and figurative free ride on many of the risky behaviors they suggest. They can "egg on" a teen driver to take some dangerous action, knowing that they won't experience most of the consequences directly, because they are almost certain not to bear any legal responsibility for anything bad that happens. Peers are not only literally being driven, but they are also given a figurative "free ride" on risky behaviors—gaining the benefits without experiencing many of the costs. . . .

Specific Sources of Peer Influence

Peers engage in behaviors that constitute influences both proximal and distal to the immediate driving context. Proximal influences occur as adolescents are actually in a car driving and involve several different groups of peers, the most obvious and most widely studied group being passengers in the adolescent's vehicle. Also worth consideration, however, are "caravan peers" in adjacent cars or in vehicles the teen encounters on the road, as well as pedestrians. Exiting a school parking lot at the end of the school day, for example, adolescents may be conversing with passengers in their own car, waving or shouting to peers who are on the sidewalk or moving to other cars, and gesturing to—perhaps even talking on a cell phone with—a driver in a car ahead of or behind their own. Each group of peers provides an opportunity for distinct influences on driver behavior, as well as the potential of interactive influences. Peers, for example, may encourage a driver to speed up and negotiate a dangerous pass so that they can yell something to passengers in the car ahead of them.

Negative Peer Influences

Negative peer influences that are proximal to the driving context can occur through a variety of behaviors. Passengers may passively distract drivers simply by talking with them when teens need to focus full attention on the task of driving. . . . Drivers may also encounter active distraction from peers playing music loudly, engaging in conversations that heighten emotions, or doing other things that more directly draw an adolescent's attention away from the task of navigating the car. Virtually all of the participants (94%) in a recent national survey of adolescents' perceptions of teen driving reported observing passengers distracting the driver in some way. Research is now needed to examine the relationship of such acts of distraction to the occurrence of motor vehicle crashes. Even more worrisome are acts of *disruption* that directly interfere with driving, such as a passenger grabbing the steering wheel or nudging a driver, a pedestrian feigning a lunge in front of the teen's car, or a caravan driver "cutting off" a teen on the road. A final negative influence category is *incitement,* when peers' words or behavior encourage risky driving. Incitement occurs, for instance, when a teen navigating one car zooms past another car with a menacing wave to the driver, whose passengers enthusiastically scream at their driver to catch up and "pass him back." Rates of such behavior are not well documented, but one Australian study indicates that drivers report being incited by youthful passengers (aged 16–24 years) more often than by adults. The risk to teenage drivers and passengers would be especially high in circumstances where these various types of influence coalesce and build on each other, such as when teens leave unchaperoned social gatherings involving alcohol. Future research might consider whether this is one of the reasons that motor vehicle crash rates for teenagers are much higher on weekends with passengers in the car than under other circumstances.

Positive Peer Influences

Peers also engage in proximal positive influences on teen drivers. This can occur through *modeling* of positive behaviors, such as when the driver in the lead car in a caravan of vehicles sets a prudent pace and maintains a safe driving distance from other vehicles. *Positive reinforcement* is another form of a positive influence process, encompassing instances, for example, when adolescents make positive comments about a teen's safe driving, which then becomes more consistent. Little is known about the incidence rates of such behaviors because investigators rarely ask about them. However, in a study of Norwegian adolescents, [P.] Ulleberg reported that young women challenge the behavior of unsafe drivers more often than young men do, and that the willingness to chide peers for risky driving is a function of personality dispositions (sensation seeking), attitudes about unsafe driving, and confidence that a driver will heed one's remonstrations.

Complementing these positive and negative forms of influence in the immediate driving context are several types of influence more distal from that context. These involve interactions with peers outside of the driving situation which can affect an adolescent's behavior behind the wheel. Again, these peer influences can enhance or disrupt responsible driving by teens.

Risky driving was more common among male than female teens.

One mode of distal influence is *storytelling*, in which an adolescent recounts an incident for peers that involves a driving episode. If the story emphasizes the fun and excitement of a dangerous driving incident or the approval and involvement of admired peers, it is likely to encourage risk taking by those who hear it. However, if the story features more-negative overtones, it may discourage risky driving. Such stories may be accompanied by a second mode of distal influence—*norm setting*—in which teens discuss or debate acceptable patterns of behavior within their group. Most studies that have considered distal peer influences involve drinking and driving. Several investigators, for example, found that adolescents were less likely to drive under the influence of alcohol, or to ride with drivers who had been drinking, if they perceived that their peers disapproved of this behavior.

Gender differences are a prominent theme throughout the research on peer influences. In a well designed observational study that exemplifies these differences, [B.] Simons-Morton et al. reported that risky driving was more common among male than female teens. Risk was exacerbated when male drivers were accompanied by a male passenger, but it was reduced to nonsignificance and almost reversed when they were driving with a female passenger. Other demographic characteristics (e.g., ethnic or socioeconomic background, urbanicity) are virtually ignored in all of this research.

In terms of future research, several types of knowledge are seriously needed. First, we know remarkably little about the nature and quality of peer interactions that actually take place within cars. Technologies that allow these interactions to be monitored are now available and can help identify not simply the ways in which peers heighten driving risks, but also the conditions in which peer interactions do not heighten risks or perhaps even reduce them. Similarly, research is needed on the qualities of adolescents who are most and least at risk from such peer influences. Longitudinal studies of adolescent development routinely track other high-risk behaviors (e.g., sexual and criminal behavior), yet rarely tap driving behaviors that may create even greater health risks.

A Ray of Hope

Is there a ray of hope amidst this perfect storm of factors that lead to risky teen driving? We believe so. Approaches that seek to alter the nature of peer influences (e.g., promoting "skillful copiloting"), reduce peer influences (e.g., enhancing refusal skills), or redirect peer influences more positively (e.g., increasing the value within the peer group of being crash-free) all warrant attention. One important feature of a perfect storm is that its power is largely dependent on many unique elements being present simultaneously. Remove even one or two of the elements, and the power of the storm is greatly diminished. From that perspective, the lengthiness of the list of risk factors presented above, rather than serving as a basis for pessimism, may give real reason for hope in offering many potential targets for efforts to reduce risks and enhance protective factors associated with adolescent driving. Future research is now needed to examine whether such efforts may indeed lead to significant reductions in the risks associated with adolescent driving.

6

Teen Peers Can Influence Safe Driving Habits

Stephen Wallace

Stephen Wallace is senior adviser for policy, research, and educa-tion at SADD (Students Against Destructive Decisions) and has extensive experience as a school psychologist and adolescent counselor. He is also associate research professor and director of the Center for Adolescent Research and Education (CARE) at Susquehanna University in Pennsylvania and the author of Re-ality Gap: Alcohol, Drugs, and Sex—What Parents Don't Know and Teens Aren't Telling.

Teens hold great sway over the actions of their peers. Speaking up to protect each other, as evidenced in the successful "Friends Don't Let Friends Drive Drunk" campaign in the 1980s and 1990s, saves lives. Warnings from a friend about the dangers of reckless and distracted driving—including speeding, talking on a cell phone, and text messaging—carries weight.

*F*riends Don't Let Friends Drive Drunk was once the rallying cry for an army of young people campaigning to curb im-paired driving among their peers. In it lies a simple proposi-tion: that friends have a special responsibility to keep each other safe and alive.

And it worked!

Stephen Wallace, "The Gift of a Lifetime: Friends Don't Let Friends Drive Dangerously," Students Against Destructive Decisions, December 8, 2009. Stephen Wallace, senior ad-visor at SADD (Students Against Destructive Decisions) and director of the Center for Adolescent Research and Education (CARE) at Susquehanna University, has broad expe-rience as a school psychologist and adolescent counselor. © Summit Communications Management Corporation 2009. All Rights Reserved.

From the early eighties to the mid-nineties, alcohol-related crash deaths among youth plummeted by 60 percent. Thousands and thousands of lives saved through the selfless act of speaking up to protect another.

What a concept.

And one that research from SADD (Students Against Destructive Decisions) and Liberty Mutual Insurance suggests could play an equally effective role in decreasing other threats to young drivers—and passengers—on the roadway.

A clear majority of teen drivers say they would change their habits if their friends asked them to.

What are those threats and how prevalent are they? According to SADD and Liberty Mutual:

- 91 percent of teens say they speed;

- 90 percent talk on a cell phone while driving; and

- 73 percent read and send text messages while driving.

Yikes!

And what about the passengers?

Well, almost the exact same percentages report riding in cars with drivers who engage in those behaviors behind the wheel.

That's the bad news.

The good news is that a clear majority of teen drivers say they would change their habits if their friends asked them to:

- Speeding: 79 percent

- Talking on a cell phone: 68 percent

- Text messaging: 89 percent

Unfortunately, many teens are reluctant to speak up when a friend is driving dangerously. For example, less than half report they would say something to the driver about speeding (41 percent), talking on a cell phone (18 percent), or text messaging (46 percent).

Further complicating this already complicated problem is the fact that teens are experiencing significant physical changes in their brains (pruning of gray matter)—particularly in areas linked to the processing of information and judgment.

Marisa Silveri, Ph.D., of the Neuroimaging Center at McLean Hospital in Massachusetts points out that it is during this very time that a young person's ability to "put the brakes on" quick, less thought-out responses may be compromised.

All the more reason the voice of a friend can be lifesaver.

Speak Up or Else

It's time to change some social norms once again, just like almost thirty years ago when young people forcefully rebranded impaired driving as decidedly "uncool."

Social norms, being the commonly held or understood expectations for behavior, are powerful tools through which we define appropriate beliefs, thoughts and, perhaps most important, behaviors. Conforming to those norms is one way teens seek inclusion—as opposed to exclusion—from the all-important peer group.

Remaining connected to one's peer group and, more to the point, accepted by it is a significant motivator for teens embarking on the long journey of establishing an identity to call their own, becoming independent from Mom and Dad, and developing close, more adult-like relationships with others their age.

Through the "Speak Up or Else" campaign sponsored by the Ad Council and a coalition of state attorneys general and consumer protection agencies, young people are encouraged to change social norms related to driving behaviors by, well, saying *something*!

The campaign asks, "Why speak up?" And answers, "Because reckless driving is the no. 1 killer of 15- to 20-year-olds."

A key point of the campaign is to make sure that young people understand that how they communicate is up to them, as most kids likely don't want to appear preachy or alarmist. Saying things in their own way works just as well, probably better, than someone else's way.

Whatever way, the scourge of distracted, dangerous driving among teens must be addressed—and who better to address it than teens themselves? And at what better time?

7

Girls Are Driving More Aggressively than Previously Thought

Joseph B. White and Anjali Athavaley

Joseph B. White, a senior editor at the Wall Street Journal *(WSJ), writes the Eyes on the Road column for the WSJ. He oversees coverage of energy, transportation, environmental policy, and technology issues from the WSJ's Washington, DC, bureau. The Pulitzer Prize winner spent years covering the auto industry. Anjali Athavaley is a reporter at the* Wall Street Journal *who covers topics ranging from consumer product safety to lifestyle trends.*

Young women were conventionally thought to be more responsible drivers than young men. But a survey from the Allstate Foundation finds that teenage girls say they are taking more risks behind the wheel. Teens also said their friends drive even worse than they do. Others, however, say the results may be skewed because the study relied on what teens said about themselves and others, not on what really happens once they are in the driver's seat.

Some big auto insurers are raising the rates they charge to cover teenage girls, reflecting the crumbling of conventional wisdom that young women are more responsible behind the wheel.

In a survey of teenage drivers, Allstate Insurance Co. found that 48% of girls said they are likely to drive 10 miles per hour over the speed limit. By comparison, 36% of the boys admitted to speeding. Of the girls, 16% characterized their own driving as aggressive, up from 9% in 2005. And just over half of the girls said they are likely to drive while talking on a phone or texting, compared to 38% of the boys.

The results were "a surprise to many people," says Meghann Dowd of the Allstate Foundation, an independent charitable organization funded by Allstate, which sponsored the survey.

[Insurance] rates for teenage girls and boys are more similar than in years past.

Friends Drive Worse

While teens fessed up about their own bad behavior, they also said their friends drive even worse. The study found that 65% of the respondents, male and female, said they are confident in their own driving skills, but 77% said they had felt unsafe when another teen was driving. Only 23% of teens agree that most teens are good drivers. This suggests teens recognize in their friends the dubious and dangerous behavior they won't admit to indulging in themselves.

The data was gleaned from online interviews with 1,063 teens across the country. It was conducted in May 2009 for the Allstate Foundation by the TRU division of TNS Custom Research Inc., a Chicago-based youth research and marketing firm.

The survey relies on what teens report about themselves, and Allstate Foundation spokeswoman Meghann Dowd says that means the results could be affected by how forthcoming individuals are when answering the survey questions.

The study is a successor to a 2005 Allstate survey that also raised alarms about teenage driving, and suggested that the physiology of young brains made teens more resistant to the messages of conventional safe driving programs.

At Allstate, the new survey has prompted questions about whether the narrowing of the bad driving gender gap reflects something bigger about the way girls view themselves and their aspirations. Young women "are taking on more risks in all aspects of their lives," says Stacy Sharpe, Allstate's assistant vice president for federal affairs. Some psychologists and others who work with teenage girls say aggressive driving may be part of an overall shift toward greater assertiveness by young women, as they make big strides in everything from academics to sports.

Allstate says it won't use the new survey data to set rates for teens. Instead, rates are set based on claims experience and other factors. The company uses the survey results in its efforts to promote safer driving by teens.

But Allstate does say that rates for teenage girls and boys are more similar than in years past: "It would be fair to say the gap is closing," says spokesman Raleigh Floyd.

Still, teenage girls continue to be a better risk than boys, according to Allstate's claims data, he says.

State Farm, the nation's largest insurance company, says that currently its auto coverage premiums for teenage boys are about 40% higher than for girls. In 1985, that gap was about 61%, says Vicki Harper, a spokeswoman for State Farm, which has more than 42 million auto policies. Most girls still get a break on premiums, she says, but "their premium rates reflect there isn't as much of a difference as the rate for a teenage boy."

Indeed, a search for a quote . . . on Progressive Direct Insurance Co.'s website for two hypothetical 19-year-old drivers (one male and one female) whose choice of car, personal details (including a speeding ticket within the past three years) and coverage limits were the same, yielded prices that were very close: The girl was quoted $2,627 for six months of coverage. The boy would have paid $2,938 for six months.

Declining Fatalities

Car accidents are the leading cause of death for U.S. teenagers, according to government statistics. But accident rates have plummeted in recent years, even as the proliferation of digital devices has added a huge new source of distractions.

Overall, the U.S. Department of Transportation [DOT] says 4,054 teenagers aged 13 to 19 died in auto accidents (as both passengers and drivers) in 2008, down 54% from 1975. Boys account for about two-thirds of teens killed in vehicle accidents, but the DOT says fatalities among boys have declined 59% since 1975, faster than the 38% decline for girls.

Driver education instructors say girls and boys are still different behind the wheel—even if the notion that girls tend to be "cautious" and boys "reckless" no longer applies.

"Girls have a tendency to be a little bit more impatient," says Kathy Clausen, vice president and general manager at A-Adams School of Driving in Morton Grove, Ill. "Girls, when they get themselves in a situation, want to honk their horn. Boys will want to physically react to it more," meaning they'll want to weave and change lanes, she says.

Some instructors say the new survey data showing girls are more aggressive than boys may be skewed.

"Trust me, boys are lying," says Adrian Mic, owner of Adrian's Driving School in Tarrytown, N.Y. "Women in general are more likely to follow the rules, in my experience," he says. But girls "don't pay attention to the speed limit. They just drive the way they feel. It doesn't mean they are aggressive."

8

Driver Education Programs Do Not Create Safe Drivers

Sharon Silke Carty

Sharon Silke Carty is a senior editor for AOL Autos. She has written about the auto industry for USA Today, *the* Wall Street Journal, *and the Associated Press.*

Graduating from driver education does not adequately prepare a teenager to take on the challenges of driving. Many schools are run by businesses, focused only on getting students to pass a test, instead of preparing them for the everyday challenges of driving. Lack of oversight and funding are partly to blame. Finding a high-quality driver education school, and supplementing it with longtime parental guidance, offers better preparation for a lifetime of safe driving.

Here's one thing parents don't know: Many driver's education programs do very little to keep your teen safe on the road.

And the government says it doesn't believe driver's education is effective at all at making teens better drivers.

"Despite widespread appeal of driver education, scientific evaluations indicate that it does not produce safer drivers," the National Highway Traffic Safety Administration [NHTSA] said in a 2009 report. "Although it may be 'common sense' to think that driver education is the preferred way to learn how to

Sharon Silke Carty, "Teen Driving: Think Driving Schools Make Safe Drivers? Think Again," Autos.aol.com, September 14, 2011. Content © 2012 AOL Inc. AOL and the AOL logo are trademarks of AOL Inc. Used with permission.

drive, the notion that a traditional driver education course can by itself produce safer drivers is optimistic."

Given how easy it is to pass a driving test in the U.S., most driver's education programs are nothing more than a basic lesson in how to handle a car.

Parents need to know ... what skills their child will and won't learn in driver's ed, and make up the difference on their own.

One of the biggest struggles teen safety advocates have is driver education: Driving schools are often run by smaller business owners and are loosely regulated. Public schools have mostly backed out of driver education. And the funding that could improve programs just isn't there, primarily because there is only spotty evidence that driver's ed works.

It's a chicken-and-egg kind of problem that will keep repeating until legislators decide it's time to tackle the issue and insist states improve driver education to where it is proved beneficial and worth supporting with tax dollars.

NHTSA has recently introduced standards that could help states improve driver's education, spelling out exactly what should be taught and emphasized. But they are not mandatory rules, and it could take years for those standards to trickle down from the federal government to states.

Until then, parents need to know how to find a good school, know what skills their child will and won't learn in driver's ed, and make up the difference on their own.

Not all driving education is bad. Some schools are awful and some are excellent. Some will teach your teen how to really think about staying safe on the road, and others will spend hours of their precious training time just teaching them to parallel park—what many say is the toughest part of the driver test for a new driver. Some will teach your children how to get out of a skid, and where to put their eyes in a panic situation, while others will boast about how many of their students have passed the state driver's test (which is a terrible indicator of driving skill).

"Those programs aren't doing as well as they could be because they are so focused on passing the driving test, not on giving teens the skills they need to keep them safe," says Troy Costales, vice chairman of the Governor's Highway Safety Association and the head of the Oregon highway safety office.

The best schools use nationally-recognized textbooks, focusing much of their energy on classroom-based instruction.

Driving schools make it tempting for parents not to question the status quo: They often pick kids up right from school and drop them off at home. They often drive kids through the same route they'll take on the driving test, to make sure their students don't fail. Anyone who has spent a morning enduring the hassle of the Department of Motor Vehicles (DMV) does not want to have to go through that more than once.

"You would not believe the number of parents who don't want to come to our driving school because we won't pick kids up at home," says Debbie Prudhomme, owner of Training Wheels Driver Education in Minnesota and head of the Driving Schools Association of the Americas. "Parents just don't understand."

There is a wide variety of quality offered in private driving schools, Prudhomme says. And bigger doesn't necessarily mean better. Some of the smaller schools can offer better training than larger schools, which may be more focused on profit. Prudhomme says the best schools use nationally-recognized textbooks, focusing much of their energy on classroom-based instruction. They offer checklists kids can bring home to their parents to show what skills the student is mastering and which need to be improved. And they don't waste precious instruction time driving from house to house, picking up students in their driveways.

Tim Reeter of Glen Carbon, Ill., was basically happy with the driving school his 15-year-old son Cole attended. But he says there are still huge gaps in his skill level:

"They don't teach kids how to brake, so that's been something he's still learning," Reeter said. "And when he's taking off, I have to remind him he doesn't have to go from zero to the speed limit immediately."

And stopping still seems to be an issue, with Cole rolling through stop signs and sometimes failing to fully stop. Reeter has taken responsibility for a large portion of his son's driving education.

"I think he's a really good driver, I feel really comfortable with him behind the wheel," Reeter said. "It's great for me, he drives everywhere we go."

For "nuclear" families, that is a common approach. But such parental attention is not always possible for single-parent families, or for new immigrant families.

The Dark Ages

Over the past 30 years, there have been two significant developments affecting driver's education in the U.S.—one that plunged driving schools into a national dark ages, and a sad fatal accident 28 years later that will hopefully spark a renaissance.

Struggling with accident data that showed teens accounted for one-third of fatal accidents on the road, traffic safety and road planning officials in the 1970s wanted to know what was going on.

A couple of studies came out blaming driver's education: One, conducted by the Insurance Institute for Highway Safety, said the increasing popularity of driving education in schools was to blame, because it was putting too many teens on the road. They estimated that 80% of teens who had driver's licenses would never be driving if they hadn't had easy access to education.

Then in 1976, a group called Batelle Columbus Laboratories was asked to conduct a study of 16,000 drivers in DeKalb County, Ga., for the National Highway Traffic Safety Administration. One group of students was given 70 hours of classroom, simulation training and on-road lessons. The second group received only minimal training to pass their driver's test. And the third group received no training at all.

The study found there was little difference between all three groups: They had similar accident rates. The only major difference they found was gender. Females had lower rates of crashes than males.

A Monumental Effect

The study had a monumental effect on driver's education. Instead of revamping driver's ed to make sure it was effective, it was essentially gutted. With no evidence the programs actually worked, cash-strapped public schools began dropping their programs, leaving the work to the private sector.

And for the most part, private driving schools are only loosely regulated. In some states, there are several regulatory bodies that are responsible for driving schools. Ironically, but perhaps not surprising, such bureaucracy results in less regulation, because the process for overseeing is often confusing and muddled. No one tells driving schools what to teach, or checks up to make sure they are actually teaching safe driving behavior.

That's the way it was until a Montana crash in 2003 got folks in Washington [DC] thinking about driver's ed again.

On Jan. 23, 2003, 49-year-old Robert Selles, a teacher from Manhattan Christian School in Belgrade, Mont., loaded up a beige 1997 Oldsmobile Achieva with three students from his driving instruction class. The sky was clear, but snow earlier in the day had left slushy patches on the road.

The sun was low in the sky, and patches of the road that were in the shade of trees were quickly turning into black ice.

Montana is a snowy state. Driver's ed rules said students should still be taken out on the road during inclement weather. After all, that's the kind of situation they could face when they get their license.

Experts now are gathering evidence to show that good driver's ed programs make a difference.

Erik Eekhoff, 14, was behind the wheel. It was his third of ten lessons on the road. Two other passengers, also 14, were in the back seat. A large teal green delivery truck was heading their way down Route 347, a two-lane road just outside Belgrade. The driver said he saw the car heading towards him, going no more than 35 or 45 mph.

Then he saw the car fishtail, the truck driver told NTSB [National Transportation Safety Board] investigators. It swerved into his lane. He tried to avoid the car by steering left, but hit the car on the passenger side.

Everyone inside the Oldsmobile died at the scene. The coroner said they all died from blunt force trauma and flail wounds, which is when the rib cage fractures in more than three places.

"That was the accident that got the wheels turning again," Costales said. "The NTSB said, 'Hey, what's going on with driver's ed?' And now we're talking about it again."

What Works

Experts now are gathering evidence to show that good driver's ed programs make a difference. In Oregon, Costales says his state's program is showing results.

In Oregon, the state mandates teen drivers get 50 hours of practice behind the wheel with an adult. Then they can choose to either do another 50 hours behind the wheel, or take a formal driver's ed program.

The teens who take driver's ed are getting to 10% to 12% fewer crashes, and getting 20% to 30% fewer citations. The state is one of just a handful that closely regulate and monitor driving programs.

Mike Speck, lead instructor at Ford's Driving Skills For Life—a free program offered over select weekends in 30 cities—starts his speech by telling the teens what a great driver he is. The former race car driver uses his resume to build credibility with teens. He's not afraid to let them know that he really loves driving and that he knows it can be fun to go fast.

"But the number one skill I want them to walk away with is the ability to make the right decisions," he said. "The decisions they make behind the wheel really seal their fate."

9

Brain Development Limits the Decision-Making Skills of Teen Drivers

Laurence Steinberg

Laurence Steinberg, a distinguished professor of psychology at Temple University, is the author of You and Your Adolescent: The Essential Guide for Ages 10–25. *He chaired the National Academies Committee on the Science of Adolescence in 2010.*

Inexperience is not the sole reason automobile accidents are the leading cause of death and disability for teenagers. Science also plays a key role. Scientists are using imaging technology to see inside the brain and watch what happens when adolescents weigh reward versus risk. The prefrontal cortex, which helps process complex decisions, undergoes massive changes during adolescence. Brain immaturity is the reason teens cannot properly gauge danger in the face of achieving pleasure and excitement. For teens, nothing stands in the way of the pursuit of pleasure until the brain matures and is able to balance risk and reward.

Most people are well aware automobile crashes are the leading cause of death and disability for adolescents. But there are many misconceptions about why adolescent drivers have proportionately more crashes than adults. They are of course less experienced, but this is not the whole story, because even when drivers of similar experience are com-

Laurence Steinberg, "Brain Development Science Sheds Light on Teen Driving," *Edmunds Auto Observer*, February 25, 2011. All rights reserved. Reprinted by permission of the author.

pared, teenagers still have more crashes than adults. Nor is drinking the explanation—in fact, alcohol accounts for a far smaller proportion of car accidents among adolescents than among older drivers. What studies show is reckless driving—driving too fast, driving while distracted, failing to take into account the dangers associated with driving in bad conditions, and the like—is by and large the main contributor to teen automobile crashes.

Before the development of brain-imaging technology, scientists could only speculate about the workings of the adolescent brain.

The conventional answer to this problem has been driver education—coursework designed to familiarize adolescents with the rules of the road and the principles of safe driving. But experts now agree education alone may not solve the problem. In the case of reckless driving, as with many other forms of risk-taking, teens usually know they are driving in a way that is potentially dangerous. (In fact, many define "safe driving" as being able to drive recklessly without having an accident!) I've spoken to many parents who tell stories of how their teen willingly drove 100 miles an hour just to see what it felt like, or tried to take a curve at breakneck speed, just to see if he could do it. Why would someone knowingly drive in a way that contradicts everything he or she has been taught about driver safety?

In recent years, scientists have increasingly turned to the study of adolescent brain development for answers. Before the development of brain-imaging technology, scientists could only speculate about the workings of the adolescent brain. Now, however, using the same scanners that identify torn ligaments and tumors, researchers are able to see inside adolescents' brains and watch what happens when they think. We now know that, other than the first three years of life, no period of development is characterized by more-dramatic brain changes than adolescence. The specific nature of these changes helps explain why adolescents may be especially inclined toward risky behavior.

The area in the very front of the brain (the prefrontal cortex, which sits behind your forehead and between your temples) is the brain's CEO [chief executive officer]. It is active when we are thinking complicated thoughts—weighing alternatives, calculating risks and rewards, constructing a plan, making complex decisions. And this is where some of the most important brain changes take place during adolescence. By the end of adolescence, brain activity in the prefrontal cortex is more efficient, and communication between it and other parts of the brain—especially those related to the way we experience and perceive emotions, rewards, and threats—is better. The maturation of the prefrontal cortex results in improvements in skills such as logical reasoning, planning ahead, and thinking about several different things at once. Although these improvements don't occur overnight, there are noticeable changes in the way adolescents think. Compared with preadolescents, adolescents' brains work better and faster.

Continuing Brain Maturation

Brain maturation doesn't end in adolescence, though. Imaging studies show the brain is still maturing well into the mid-20s, especially in regions responsible for regulating emotions, controlling impulses, and balancing risk and reward. Psychologists draw a distinction between "cold" cognition (when we are thinking about something that doesn't have much emotional content, such as how to solve an algebra problem) and "hot" cognition (when we are thinking about something that can make us feel exuberant or excited, angry or depressed, such as whether to go joyriding with friends or throw a punch at someone who insulted a girlfriend). The systems of the brain responsible for cold cognition are mature by age 16. But the systems that control hot cognition aren't—they are still developing well into the 20s. That's why the teen who gets straight A's in school can also do such dumb things when out with buddies—like drive in ways he or she knows are dangerous.

There is more dopamine activity in the brain's reward center in early adolescence than at any other time of life.

At the same time the adolescent brain is maturing in ways that enable a teen to become more capable of reasoned thinking, it is also changing in ways that encourage risky behavior. Do you remember how good your first passionate kiss felt? How much you loved the music of your youth? How hard you laughed with your high school friends? Things that feel good, feel better during adolescence. Scientists now understand why.

A chemical in the brain called dopamine is responsible for the feeling of pleasure. When something enjoyable happens, we experience what some scientists have called a "dopamine squirt," which leads to the sensation of pleasure. It makes us want whatever elicited the squirt, because the feeling of pleasure it produces is so strong.

Seeking Pleasure

We now know there is a rapid increase in dopamine activity in early adolescence—in fact, there is more dopamine activity in the brain's reward center in early adolescence than at any other time of life. Because things feel especially pleasurable during early adolescence, young adolescents go out of their way to seek rewarding experiences. At all ages we seek out things that make us feel good, of course. But the push to do this is much more intense in early adolescence than before or after.

The urge to seek out rewarding and pleasurable experiences is a mixed blessing. On the plus side, it's part of what makes it so much fun to be a teenager. But sometimes this drive is so intense adolescents can exhibit a sort of reward "tunnel vision." They are so driven to seek pleasure they may not pay attention to the associated risks. To a teenager, the anticipation of driving fast can feel so good thoughts about a speeding ticket (or worse) don't even make it onto the radar.

Heeding Vulnerability

This combination of advanced (but not yet mature) reasoning and heightened sensation seeking explains why otherwise-intelligent adolescents often do things that are surprisingly foolish (like driving 100 miles an hour just to see what it feels like). More important, the fact that teens' ability to control impulses is immature just when interest in sensation seeking is stronger than ever makes them vulnerable to making mistakes.

Graduated driving laws have been successful in part because they prevent teen drivers from putting themselves in situations that exacerbate their vulnerability to risk taking. In our own research, we have found the mere presence of friends elevates risky decision-making among teenagers, but has no such impact on adults. We have shown this effect is due to the impact friends have on the adolescent brain's reward system. When friends are around, this system is more easily aroused, and teens then pay more attention to the potential rewards of a risky decision than to the potential costs. This helps explain why rates of automobile crashes among teen drivers are so much higher when they have passengers than when they are driving alone. And it reaffirms how important it is for you and your adolescent to have an ongoing conversation about the importance of putting the brakes on thrill-seeking when he or she is behind the wheel. Tell them to save that for roller coasters.

19

Firm Parents Keep Teen Drivers Safe

Serena Gordon

Serena Gordon is an award-winning journalist for HealthDay News. Her reports on health, family, and children's issues have appeared in US Department of Health and Human Services newsletters and publications such as the Washington Post *and* US News & World Report.

Parents who are actively involved in their teen's safety behind the wheel can cut their child's chances of being in an accident by 50 percent and decrease the chance their child will drink and drive. An authoritative parenting style, combining high support along with rules and monitoring, is the most effective approach. Limiting access to a car also holds a teen more accountable and keeps the lines of communication open between parent and child. Children with parents who are permissive or uninvolved are more likely to be free-wheeling drivers who do not wear seat belts and who drink and drive, among other risky behaviors.

Your parenting style can make a huge difference in your teen's safety once he or she gets behind the wheel of a car.

Parents who set firm rules, but do so in a helpful, supportive way, can reduce the likelihood of their teen getting into an auto accident by half and decrease rates of drinking and driving, two new studies find. Positive rule-setting can also increase the odds a teen will wear a seatbelt and lessen the likelihood of talking or texting on a cell phone while driving.

"Parent involvement really matters. Active parenting can save teenagers' lives," said Dr. Kenneth Ginsburg, an adolescent medicine specialist at the Center for Injury Research and Prevention at the Children's Hospital of Philadelphia. "Parents who give rules, set boundaries and monitor those boundaries with warmth and support can have a really dramatic effect on teen driving safety."

Ginsburg is the lead author of two studies published online in *Pediatrics* on Sept. 28 [2009]. Both studies were sponsored by State Farm Insurance.

The first study looked at the association between parenting styles and teen driving behaviors and attitudes, while the second assessed teen behavior based on their access to a vehicle.

Parental Influence

The first study included a nationally representative sample of 5,665 teens in 9th through 11th grades. Parenting style was reported by the teens and fell into one of four categories: authoritative (high support along with rules and monitoring); authoritarian (low support with rules and monitoring), permissive (high support with low rules and monitoring), and uninvolved (low support and low rules).

Teens who had authoritative or authoritarian parents wore seatbelts twice as often as teens with uninvolved parents. Teens with parents in these groups were also half as likely to speed as those with uninvolved parents. Teens with authoritative parents—high support and rules—were half as likely to get into a car accident, 71 percent less likely to drink and drive, and 29 percent less likely to talk or text on their cell phones while driving compared to teens with uninvolved parents.

The second study included 2,167 teens and found that 70 percent had "primary access" to a vehicle. That didn't necessarily mean that the teens had their own cars, Ginsburg said, but it could mean they had easy access to the keys and didn't need to ask permission to take a family car.

There are clear rules that must always be followed, and rules that will change as your teen gains experience and demonstrates responsibility.

After controlling the data to account for the extra hours these teens likely spent behind the wheel, the researchers found that teens with easy access to a vehicle were more than twice as likely to crash, about 25 percent more likely to use a cell phone while driving and about 25 percent more likely to speed than teens who had to ask permission to use a car.

Why the difference? Ginsburg said he suspects it's because teens with easy access to a car don't necessarily feel as accountable. They don't have anyone asking where they're going or whom they'll be with. "They miss out on that conversation and appropriate monitoring," he said.

Parents should control the keys to the car for at least the first six to 12 months of driving, he added.

Rules Can Change over Time

Ginsburg said there are clear rules that must always be followed, and rules that will change as your teen gains experience and demonstrates responsibility.

Clear rules include:

- Always wear your seatbelt.

- Never speed.

- Never drink and drive.

- Never drive fatigued.

- Never use your cell phone or text while driving.

Rules that can change as your child gains experience and skill include having passengers, driving at night, increased access to the car and driving in bad weather. Ginsburg said it's important to make sure there's a reward for your teen for good driving behavior. "There has to be something in it for them," he said.

"Teens do need parents to set rules, and there need to be consequences when the rules aren't followed," said Dr. Barbara Gaines, director of the trauma and injury prevention program at Children's Hospital of Pittsburgh.

"Parents need to know that the moment a child gets a driver's license is the riskiest time in their lives. Don't treat this time as a fait accompli. Getting the license is a goal, and the first step in a process," she said.

Most parents worry more about sex, drugs and drinking than they do about driving, but car crashes are the biggest threat to teen safety, Ginsburg added. "The great news is that parents really matter. And, when you stay involved and do so in a way that promotes safety, not control, driving becomes the greatest opportunity to promote their children's safety."

11

Monitoring Devices Benefit Teen Drivers

Insurance Institute for Highway Safety

The Insurance Institute for Highway Safety is a nonprofit, scientific, and educational organization dedicated to reducing deaths, injuries, and property damage from highway crashes. The institute is supported by auto insurers.

Monitoring devices help parents tag along when their teenagers get behind the wheel. The devices alert drivers to hazards like speeding, not wearing a seat belt, and driving aggressively. Studies found the gadgets helped ease parents' minds and gave teen drivers the chance to learn from their mistakes, but success requires cooperation and dedication.

When parents are watching, their teenage children drive differently than when they're alone or with friends. Unsupervised teens take more risks behind the wheel. A new [Insurance Institute for Highway Safety] study indicates that equipping the cars teens drive with in-vehicle monitoring devices can help reduce these risks by giving feedback about driving behavior to both teenagers and their parents. Yet the devices may turn out to be tough sells not only to the beginning drivers but even to their parents, and over time the teens may become less cautious if they think their parents aren't paying attention. A companion survey indicates that most parents think the technology helps their kids be safer drivers.

"Monitoring devices can help reduce teens' risky driving," says Anne McCartt, Institute senior vice president for research, "and perhaps ease some of the worry parents face when their kids start to drive. Our findings also suggest that technology can't substitute for parents getting involved."

Vehicles driven by the 84 teens in the study were outfitted with a black box that continuously monitored their driving.

Teenage drivers' crash risk is consistently higher than the risk in any other age group. One proven way to reduce this risk is through strong graduated licensing laws. Another potential way is to use technologies to monitor driving and flag risky behavior like speeding, aggressive driving, and nonuse of belts. Some of these gadgets can pinpoint a vehicle's location and even let parents dial directly into the car if an alert sounds. Several insurers offer such devices to policyholders with teen drivers.

"When I'm with her my daughter drives differently than when she's with her friends," says Kathy Paxton, mom of a teenager who participated in the study that monitored 16- and 17-year-old drivers in the suburban Washington, DC, area during a 24-week period. "You really don't know how they're driving until you have a monitor in their car. It was an eye opener. I would love to have my other daughter who's going to be driving soon have it in her car."

Vehicles driven by the 84 teens in the study were outfitted with a black box that continuously monitored their driving. The unit had global positioning system capabilities plus a satellite modem to transmit data to a central processing center. The device recorded driving-specific data but no video or sound. It detected when drivers braked sharply or accelerated suddenly, didn't use belts, and exceeded speed limits. Data were posted on a secure website for parents to review.

Participants were randomly assigned to 1 of 4 groups. Drivers in groups 1 and 2 heard audible alerts for risky maneuvers. A short, low-pitched buzz sounded for sudden braking and acceleration. A continuous low-pitched buzz sounded when the belt wasn't buckled and stopped only when it was fastened. Speeding triggered a single beep at 2.5 mph over the posted limit, followed by continuous beeps at increasing pitch and frequency when the teenage drivers exceeded the limit by more than 10 mph. The alerts were designed to be louder than the radio and the surrounding traffic.

For drivers in group 1, information about triggering events immediately was reported to the website for parents' inspection. Teenagers in group 2 could correct their driving within 20 seconds of an alarm to avoid having the violation reported to their parents. Researchers discovered late in the study that the conditional notification mode never had been activated, though the teen drivers and their parents in this group weren't aware of the glitch.

There were no in-vehicle alerts for drivers in group 3, just website notification. Group 4 was a control group with monitoring but no alert or web notification.

Although parents of newly licensed drivers in a previous Institute survey said they wanted to know more about their teens' unsupervised driving, researchers had trouble recruiting families for the monitoring project. Teens had to be the primary drivers of the monitored vehicles, and their parents had to have web access.

A Tough Sell

"At first it was tough finding families willing to participate until we added a $500 payment to compensate them for their time," McCartt says. "Part of the problem may be that the monitoring technology is relatively new, so parents and teens weren't familiar with it. Their reluctance also signals that more widespread use of these devices may turn out to be a tough sell."

Once the devices were in 31 vehicles, researchers noted that only a handful of parents visited the website. This prompted the Institute's study coordinator to decide to send short driving report cards every 2–3 weeks to the parents of the next teens who got devices. These reports were designed with the assumption that parents would go to the website for more details about their teenagers' risky driving. However, parents receiving the reports used the website even less frequently than those in the initial group.

Sudden braking and abrupt acceleration can signal driver risk-taking or inattentiveness.

Many teens don't use safety belts, despite the lifesaving benefits. About half of 16- and 17-year-old drivers killed in crashes in 2007 weren't belted. Monitoring devices can help, the researchers found.

At 94 percent, belt use among teens in the study already was high, and the few holdouts gave in and buckled up when the continuous buzz sounded. Belt use improved even among teens in the web-access-only group. Similar effects have been observed among drivers of all ages in studies of belt reminders that chime or buzz for extended intervals when drivers don't use belts.

Stops and Starts

Sudden braking and abrupt acceleration can signal driver risk-taking or inattentiveness. In the study, rates of sudden stops and starts fell among teenagers in the monitoring groups relative to the control group, especially in vehicles with audible alerts, but the differences were statistically significant only for teens in group 1 with immediate website notification. Alerts were short and not particularly annoying. The effects were greater among teens whose parents received periodic report cards.

Driving faster than the posted speed limit was the most prevalent risky behavior. At first, speeding more than 10 mph above the limit sharply declined among teens in the 2 groups with alerts in their vehicles, but then the rates of speeding began to rise over time. Instances of speeding more than 10 mph over the posted limit were reduced significantly only when alarms sounded in the vehicles, speed-related report cards were emailed to parents, and the teenage drivers had a chance to cancel the report cards by slowing down.

Most of the teen drivers increasingly broke speed limits over time, even though violations of more than 10 mph were posted to the web for parents to see. This may be because drivers grew more at ease behind the wheel and on the roads they traveled, McCartt says. It also could be because during the study many teenagers completed the probationary period for graduated licensing, so restrictions on young passengers were lifted. Teen drivers are more likely to take risks when they're out with other teens.

Risky behavior consistently declined among teens in the second monitoring group with driving report cards. Once these teens heard in-vehicle alerts, they believed they could correct their behavior before the system tipped off their parents. Teens in the first in-vehicle alarm group had less incentive to change their behavior. By the time they heard an alarm it was too late to prevent parental notification and improve their driving report card.

What Parents and Teenagers Think

When monitoring ended, the researchers interviewed parents and teen drivers separately about their experiences. Ninety-eight percent of the parents said they'd recommend the monitoring device to other parents. When asked what they most wanted to know about their teenager's driving, parents most often said speeding (81 percent).

"I'd recommend it, especially for new drivers, for the oversight as well as the ability it gives parents to have conversations with [their children] about what might have been going on in the car" to trigger a web alert, says David Heyman, a Maryland father whose son participated in the study.

Teens felt the device made them better drivers. Eighty-three percent in the 2 in-vehicle alert groups and 81 percent in the web-access-only group thought the device was effective. More than half in each alert group described the beeps and buzzes as annoying, and the majority were happy when the unit was removed.

12

Cell Phones and Texting Endanger Teen Drivers

Nancy Mann Jackson

Nancy Mann Jackson is a reporter who specializes in business and home and family issues.

Driver distraction is a national problem. Talking on a cell phone or texting causes drivers to lose their focus, often with deadly consequences. Driving is not a time to multitask, especially if the driver is a teenager. Nearly 28 percent of all vehicle crashes can be tied to talking on a cell phone or texting, according to the National Safety Council. Legislators and others are speaking out and taking action to curb distracted driving.

When Wil Craig tells his story, teens listen. In 2008, when he was an Indiana high school senior, Craig was riding in his girlfriend's car as she drove and texted at the same time. Distracted, she wrecked the car.

The driver had no serious injuries. But Craig suffered a collapsed lung, four broken ribs, and a traumatic brain injury. He spent eight weeks in a coma. After he learned to walk and talk again and eventually returned to school, Craig began sharing his story with other teenagers—so far more than 10,000—to help stop teen texting and driving.

Widespread Damage

There are many more people who need to hear Craig's message. Driver distraction has become a national problem, especially because cell phone use has increased. Look around the next time you're on the road (as a passenger, of course), and see how many drivers are talking or texting on their cell phones. That can lead them to take their focus off the road and cause serious, even fatal, accidents.

Nearly 28 percent of all vehicle crashes, or about 1.6 million each year, can be linked to talking on a cell phone or texting while driving, the National Safety Council estimates. The problem is especially dire for U.S. teens: Among those ages 16 and 17, some 26 percent have texted from behind the wheel. (And 43 percent of those in that age group admitted to talking on a cell phone while driving, according to a Pew Internet & American Life Project study.)

The Worst Distraction

While there are many activities that can distract a driver, such as eating or adjusting the radio while driving, sending text messages may be the worst.

"Texting is among the most dangerous activities for drivers because it involves taking your eyes and attention off the roadway," says Justin McNaull, director of state relations for AAA, formerly known as the American Automobile Association. "Even taking your eyes off the road for two seconds doubles your chances of being in a crash."

Not convinced? Stats from a Federal Motor Carrier Safety Administration study tell the story:

- Compared with 16 other distracting activities, texting had the highest odds of causing a serious crash.

- Drivers who were texting were 23.2 times more likely to crash than those drivers who weren't texting.

- When texting, drivers took their eyes off the road for an average of 4.6 seconds.

Likewise, making phone calls, even with a hands-free headset, while driving is more dangerous than speaking to a passenger. That's because a passenger will pause in conversation when the driver needs to concentrate on the road.

"Even in conversation, an adult passenger can appreciate when the driver is doing something more demanding, like merging onto the highway," McNaull says. "Someone on a cell phone doesn't know or appreciate what the driver's doing."

Driving is a new skill for teens, so doing multiple things simultaneously takes more effort for them than for more experienced drivers.

Only 2 percent of people are able to safely multitask while driving, estimates David Strayer, a psychology professor at the University of Utah. He has studied the effect that cell phone use while driving has on the brain. Even though teens are more likely to try multitasking, they're part of that 98 percent who can't do it safely, Strayer says.

Driving is a new skill for teens, so doing multiple things simultaneously takes more effort for them than for more experienced drivers.

A Rising Legal Response

As the risks of texting while driving have become more obvious, lawmakers across the country have begun to take notice—and to take action.

- Currently, laws in 30 states and the District of Columbia make it illegal to text or send e-mail while driving.

- Eight states plus the District of Columbia completely ban the use of a handheld phone while driving.

- Thirty-one states have separate restrictions for teens, including bans on using phones while driving or texting while driving.

The penalties for breaking those laws range from fines to jail time. On the federal level, texting while driving has been banned for interstate truck drivers, and Congress is considering several bills that would encourage all states to pass laws banning texting while driving.

Whether calling or texting while driving is restricted by law, smart drivers are rethinking the use of phones behind the wheel. However, it can be tough to ditch the phone.

Some teens even use technology to help them avoid texting while driving.

"People have a real desire to be connected and have the immediate ability to keep in touch with friends and family," McNaull says. "Giving up texting and talking on the phone while driving is hard."

To avoid the temptation, McNaull recommends simply turning off your phone and putting it away before getting behind the wheel. Talk to your parents, and let them know that if you don't respond to their phone calls or texts right away, it's because you're driving. Avoid calling or texting your friends if you know they're driving at the time.

Some teens even use technology to help them avoid texting while driving.

Zach Veach is a 15-year-old who races cars for Andretti Autosport. He began speaking out after a teen who had been driving for only two months was killed while texting in an accident near his home in Ohio.

To help other teens, Zach developed urTXT, an application for smart phones that sends an auto response to the sender of a text, letting the sender know that the recipient is driving and will respond later.

Like Zach, many teens are finding ways they can make a difference.

Nebraska teen Emily Reynolds says texting and driving was once a big problem among her friends. After her older sister, Cady, was killed in a crash at age 16, Emily's family started the C.A.R. Alliance for Safer Teen Driving (named for the initials of Cady Anne Reynolds). The group visits schools to share the dangers of distracted driving with those who are just beginning to drive.

Since the C.A.R. presentation at her school, Emily says, she's seen fewer and fewer classmates texting while driving. When she finds herself in a car with another teen who is texting, Emily, who's now 17, doesn't hesitate to speak up.

"I will absolutely say something, and it is usually along the lines of, 'You really shouldn't do that while you drive. Would you like me to text someone for you?'" she says. "Offering to do it for them gives a good alternative, and it gets the point across."

Zach goes even further. "The first time I see [other people] do it, I tell them that I don't want to lose my life and they don't know how dangerous texting and driving is," he says. "Most people tell me they do it all the time and nothing has happened. [If] they refuse [to stop], I turn their car off and take the keys until they agree to put the phone down."

Extreme? Maybe. But separating driving from cell phone use is a way to make sure crashes such as the one that forever changed Wil Craig's life never happen again.

Organizations to Contact

The editors have compiled the following list of organizations concerned with the issues debated in this book. The descriptions are derived from materials provided by the organizations. All have publications or information available for interested readers. The list was compiled on the date of publication of the present volume; the information provided here may change. Be aware that many organizations take several weeks or longer to respond to inquiries, so allow as much time as possible.

AAA Foundation for Traffic Safety
607 Fourteenth St. NW, Ste. 201, Washington, DC   20005
(202) 638-5944 • fax: (202) 638-5943
e-mail: info@aaafoundation.org
website: www.aaafoundation.org

The AAA Foundation is dedicated to saving lives and reducing traffic accidents. Since 1947, the nonprofit, publicly supported, charitable, educational, and research organization has funded projects to discover the causes of traffic crashes. Its website contains a wealth of information, including Keys2Drive, AAA's extensive website for teen drivers and their parents, as well as sections on distracted and aggressive driving. The site also tailors information to the viewer's state, including the state's licensing process.

Advocates for Highway and Auto Safety
750 First St. NE, Ste. 901, Washington, DC   20002
(202) 408-1711 • fax: (202) 408-1699
e-mail: advocates@saferoads.org
website: www.saferoads.org

Advocates for Highway and Auto Safety is an alliance of consumer, health, and safety groups and insurance companies that seeks to make America's roads safer. The alliance advocates the adoption of federal and state laws, policies, and programs that save lives and reduce injuries. Its website features fact sheets, news releases, polls, and reports, as well as links to legislative reports and testimony on federal legislation involving traffic safety, including issues surrounding teen driving.

Allstate Foundation
2775 Sanders Rd., F4, Northbrook, IL   60062
e-mail: grants@allstate.com
website: www.allstatefoundation.com

Since 1952, the Allstate Foundation has worked with communities to help make positive social changes, especially in the areas of teen driving and domestic violence. Its programs range from the local to the national level. The Teen Safe Driving Program encourages activism to empower adolescents to make smart choices that will reduce injuries and save lives. The website KeeptheDrive.com includes research, tips, parent-teen driving agreements, and graduated driver licensing information.

American Driver and Traffic Safety Education Association (ADTSEA)
ADTSEA/NSSP, Highway Safety Services, LLC
Indiana, PA   15705
(724) 801-8246 • fax: (724) 349-5042
e-mail: office@adtsea.org
website: www.adtsea.org

ADTSEA works with driver's education instructors worldwide and state authorities to improve driver's education standards and practices. On its website, ADTSEA publishes white papers, articles, videos, and reports covering such topics as distracted driving, driver education, drunken driving, and risk management. It also includes an online driver training program.

Century Council
2345 Crystal Dr., Ste. 910, Arlington, VA   22202
(202) 637-0077 • fax: (202) 637-0079

e-mail: info@centurycouncil.org
website: www.centurycouncil.org

Funded by American distillers, the Century Council is a non-profit, national organization committed to fighting underage drinking and drunk driving. Among the group's initiatives are the Concentration Game, which mimics distractions teen drivers may experience, and Cops in Shops, an alliance of law enforcement and retailers that works to stop illegal underage alcohol sales. Its award-winning Alcohol 101 Plus program, an interactive virtual campus, provides scenarios to help students make sensible, fact-based decisions about drinking and to learn about the consequences if they make poor choices.

Ford Driving Skills for Life (DSFL)
One American Rd., Dearborn, MI 48126
(888) 978-8765
website: www.drivingskillsforlife.com

Ford Driving Skills for Life was established in 2003 by the Ford Motor Company Fund, the Governors Highway Safety Association, and various safety experts to teach newly licensed teens the necessary skills for safe driving beyond what they learn in standard driver education programs. The DSFL helps new drivers gain proficiency by focusing on four key areas: hazard recognition, vehicle handling, speed management, and space management. The group's website offers videos, educational materials, and tips on such topics as car care, driving in inclement weather, and the dangers of speeding.

Gillian Sabet Memorial Foundation
31852 Coast Hwy., Ste. 105, Laguna Beach, CA 92651
(949) 939-1306
e-mail: foundation@gilliansabet.org
website: www.journeysafe.org

Founded in memory of two teens who died in a distracted driving accident, the Gillian Sabet Memorial Foundation focuses on teen passenger safety. The organization cites teen driver inexperience and immaturity as the leading cause of teen traffic deaths. It aims to help teens help each other by modeling safe behaviors on and off the road and by practicing positive peer pressure to prevent at-risk situations. The non-profit organization's website provides statistics and resources for both teens and parents.

Insurance Institute for Highway Safety (IIHS)

1005 N. Glebe Rd., Ste. 800, Arlington, VA 22201
(703) 247-1500 • fax: (703) 247-1588
website: www.hwysafety.org

The IIHS is a nonprofit research and public information organization funded by auto insurers. The institute conducts research to reduce deaths, injuries, and property damage from driving accidents, including those involving teen drivers, by changing driver behaviors, improving vehicle safety, and altering road design features. Its newsletter *Status Report* and teen driving laws and other regulations for every state, as well as congressional testimony on issues related to teen driving, are available on its website.

National Highway Traffic Safety Administration (NHTSA)

1200 New Jersey Ave. SE, West Bldg., Washington, DC 20590
(888) 327-4236
e-mail: www.nhtsa.dot.gov/Contact
website: www.nhtsa.dot.gov

The function of the NHTSA is to save lives, prevent injuries, and reduce economic costs due to road traffic crashes. It achieves these goals through education, research, safety standards, and enforcement activity. NHTSA directly impacts policy making and vehicle safety in the United States as well as develops standards for driver education programs. The website features NHTSA's extensive research and data. Its section on teen drivers features fact sheets, articles, and reports.

National Organizations for Youth Safety (NOYS)

7371 Atlas Walk Way, Ste. 109, Gainesville, VA   20155
(828) 367-6697 • fax: (866) 559-9398
e-mail: info@noys.org
website: www.noys.org

NOYS is a collaborative effort of national organizations, federal agencies, and business and industry leaders to promote youth safety, including traffic safety. The site's section on traffic safety resources provides statistics and other research. Texting and other forms of distracted driving are the focus of current projects.

National Safety Council (NSC)

1121 Spring Lake Dr., Itasca, IL   60143-3201
(630) 285-1121 • fax: (630) 285-1315
e-mail: info@nsc.org
website: www.nsc.org

Founded in 1913 and chartered by the US Congress in 1953, the NSC is a nonprofit, nongovernmental public service organization that relies on education and research to protect lives and promote health in the home, the workplace, and on the road. The group works with businesses, government agencies, elected officials, and others to provide education to prevent unintentional injuries and deaths. The council conducts research and provides information on highway safety. The NSC publishes the yearly *Injury Facts* and other publications on safety and health. On its website, NSC offers fact sheets on key safety issues, including teen driving, and has teen driving safety videos.

Students Against Destructive Decisions (SADD)

255 Main St., Marlborough, MA   01752
(877) SADD-INC • fax: (508) 481-5759
e-mail: info@sadd.org
website: www.saddonline.com

Formerly called Students Against Drunk Driving, SADD is now dedicated to preventing all destructive decisions that impact teen safety. The school-based organization seeks to provide students with prevention and intervention tools to build the confidence needed to make healthy choices and behavioral changes on such issues as underage drinking, impaired driving, and drug use. The website contains a wealth of information on such topics as starting local chapters, nationwide activities, and research and articles, including some specifically on teen driving research. SADD offers e-newsletters titled *ParentTeen Matters* and the *SADDvocate* and provides access to editorials and articles in its online magazine, *Teens Today*.

Traffic Injury Research Foundation (TIRF)

171 Nepean St., Ste. 200, Ottawa, ON   K2P 0B4
  Canada
(613) 238-5235 • fax: (613) 238-5292
e-mail: sarao@tirf.ca
website: www.trafficinjuryresearch.com

Founded in 1964, TIRF is an independent road safety institute that seeks to reduce traffic-related deaths and injuries worldwide by designing, promoting, and implementing effective programs and policies based on sound research. TIRF publications include brochures, the *TIRF Bulletin*, and the *Road Safety Monitor*. Technical reports, including *Investigation of Teen Driver Programs with Parental Involvement in the United States* and *Youth and Road Crashes: A Program of Research and Prevention*, are available on its website.

University of North Carolina Highway Safety Research Center

730 Martin Luther King Jr. Blvd., CB #3430
Chapel Hill, NC   27599
(919) 962-2202 • fax: (919) 962-8710
e-mail: info@hsrc.unc.edu
website: www.hsrc.unc.edu

The goal of the University of North Carolina Highway Safety Research Center is to improve the safety, security, access, and efficiency of all surface transportation modes through research, evaluation, and information dissemination. It publishes the quarterly newsletter *Directions*, recent issues of which are on its website. The site's research library section provides access to fact sheets, articles, and reports on traffic safety issues such as teen driving, including "Measuring Changes in Teenage Driver Crash Characteristics During the Early Months of Driving" and "The Transition to Unsupervised Driving."

Bibliography

Books

Phil Berardelli   *Safe Young Drivers: A Guide for Parents and Teens.* Mountain Lake Park, MD: Mountain Lake Press, 2008.

Sheryl Feinstein   *Inside the Teenage Brain: Parenting a Work in Progress.* Lanham, MD: Rowman & Littlefield, 2009.

Karen Gravelle   *The Driving Book: Everything New Drivers Need to Know but Don't Know to Ask.* New York: Walker, 2005.

Frank Miller   *Driverthink. Reality Based Driving Tips, Ideas and Suggestions for the Everyday Driver.* Indianapolis: Dog Ear, 2009.

Greg Roza   *Frequently Asked Questions About Driving and the Law.* FAQ: Teen Life. New York: Rosen, 2010.

Timothy C. Smith   *Crash-Proof Your Kids: Make Your Teen a Safer, Smarter Driver.* New York: Simon & Schuster, 2006.

Tom Vanderbilt   *Traffic: Why We Drive the Way We Do (and What It Says About Us).* New York: Knopf, 2008.

Periodicals and Internet Sources

Allstate Foundation	"License to Save Report Finds Graduated Driver Licensing Could Save 2,000 Lives and $13.6 Billion Annually; Allstate Foundation Parent-Teen Driving Agreement Helps Parents Start Safe Driving Talk," Allstate Newsroom, December 6, 2011. www.allstatenewsroom.com.
Rachel Aydt	"Danger: Behind the Wheel: Distracted Driving Is on the Rise, Making Summer the Scariest Time for Teens to Be on the Road. Here's What's Causing New Drivers to Lose Control—and the Moves Being Made to Keep Ya Safe," *Girls' Life*, August–September 2009.
Sharon Silke Carty	"Series: What Parents Should Do to Keep Teen Drivers Safe," AOL Autos, September 21, 2011. www.autos.aol.com.
Rachel Cook	"Spy Parents: AAA Rolls Out Free Program to Monitor Teen Drivers," *Bakersfield Californian*, November 13, 2011.
Larry Copeland	"Technology Tackles Teen Drivers' Phone Distractions," *USA Today*, January 17, 2012.
John DiConsiglio	"He Drove Drunk—and Someone Died," *Scholastic Choices*, September 2011.

Jill Duffy — "Six Apps for Safer Driving," *PC Magazine Online*, December 14, 2011. www.pcmag.com.

Entertainment Close-up — "State Farm: Some Parents Set Poor Example with Cell Phones, Distractions, While Teaching Teens to Drive," October 24, 2011.

Stefano Esposito — "Fewer Teens Desperate to Drive—Is the Internet the Reason?," *Chicago Sun-Times*, January 12, 2012.

Arthur Goodwin, Robert Foss, Lewis Margolis, and Martha Waller — "Parents, Teens and the Learner Stage of Graduated Driver Licensing," *AAA Foundation for Traffic Safety*, October 2010. www.aaafoundation.org.

Jim Gorzelany — "Social Media Trumps Driving Among Today's Teens," *Forbes*, January 23, 2012.

Benjamin Hoffman — "Teen Drivers: Inherent Risks, Protection Strategies," *Pediatric Annals*, November 2010.

Debra Kent — "Crash-Proof Your Teen: There's a New Way to Prep Your Child to Get Behind the Wheel. Here, the Info Every Parent Needs," *Good Housekeeping*, May 2010.

| Laura Linn | "Driving Force: These Teens Want You to Know That One of the Keys to Having a Safe and Bright Future Is to Behave Responsibly When You're in a Car," *Scholastic Choices*, September 2007. |

| Joan Lowy | "Fuel Prices Help Drive Down Traffic Fatalities, Study Finds," *Transport Topics*, September 1, 2008. |

| Kelsey Mays | "Teen Safe Driving 101: Understanding Common Mistakes Young Drivers Make Can Help Them Avoid Accidents," *Chicago Tribune*, December 4, 2011. |

| National Institutes of Health | "Graduated Drivers Licensing Programs Reduce Fatal Teen Crashes," November 4, 2011. www.nih.gov. |

| Joel Provano | "Risky Business: Teens Driving with Other Teens," *Atlanta Journal-Constitution*, January 24, 2012. |

| Sascha Segan | "The NTSB's Cell Phone Overkill," *PC Magazine Online*, December 14, 2011. www.pcmag.com. |

| Vikki Sloviter | "How Teen Behavior Influences Their Driving: National Young Driver Survey," *Pediatrics for Parents*, May 1, 2009. |

| Michael Tracey | "Dead Kids Make Bad Laws," *Reason*, June 1, 2011. |

Jim Turley   "Situational Awareness," *Sportscar*,
                            November 2010.

Stephen Wallace   "The Rearview Mirror: Driving
                            Safety at Camp," *Camping Magazine*,
                            March–April 2010.

Stephen Wallace   "Snap! How Split-Second Decisions
                            Imperil Youth," SADD, June 16, 2008.
                            www.sadd.org.

Kevin A. Wilson   "Who's Teaching the Teens? We Still
                            Have No Minimal Standard
                            Nationwide," *AutoWeek*, October 3,
                            2011.

Index